まちのうた
Impressions of Towns

公益財団法人JAL財団＝編
Edited by JAL Foundation

Berbilang kaum
berbelanja bersama
di kota raya

ブロンズ新社
Bronze Publishing

この「地球」の希望の光

建築家　安藤忠雄

ありふれた日常の中にひそむ感動を、三行の詩に託す「ハイク」。そんな刺激的な言葉のゲームに、世界の子どもたちがそれぞれの母語で参加する。創意にあふれた、実にすばらしい企画だと思います。今回のお題は「まち」。

スリランカの7歳は活気あふれる港町の喧騒を（23ページ）、ロシアの11歳は世界で最も寒い夜の街灯りの温かさを（47ページ）、ルーマニアの12歳は中世の趣ただよう森の中の迷宮都市の幻想の世界を（62ページ）——みな、それぞれの心にある「自分たちの街」を、思いおもいの言葉と画で大胆に描き出しています。その一枚一枚が生き生きと語りかけてくるようで、「私たちの生きる地球とは、こんなにも多様で、豊かなものだったのか！」と新鮮な感動を覚えます。やはり純粋でまっすぐな子どもには、大人にはない創造力がありますね。

私たちは今、気候変動、経済格差、食糧・エネルギー危機に感染症のパンデミック、終わらない戦争など、多くの複雑で困難な課題に直面しています。一方で、絶え間ない技術革新で社会は急激に変化し、世界全体が先の見えない不安な空気に包まれているようです。

そんな中でも、キラキラと輝きを失わない子どもたち。彼らの存在が、この「地球」の希望の光です。その光を絶やさぬよう、未来を創る力が育まれるよう、私たち大人は頑張らねばならない。彼らには無垢の好奇心、探求心という可能性の力があるのですから、あとはそれを受けとめ、育んでやれる場所があればいいんです。

アンドリュー・カーネギーは、莫大な財を成したあと、社会還元として世界各地に二千五百もの図書館を寄付しました。私も建築という職業を通じて、手の届く範囲でいい、育ててくれた社会に恩返しをしたい。そんな思いで【こども本の森】プロジェクトを続けています。市が準備する土地に、寄贈という形で私が建物をつくり、市民の志を原資として本を集め、運営していく。官民一体で実現する、子どものための図書施設です。地元・大阪を皮切りに、すでに三つが完成、さらに国内外で四つを計画中です。「世界こどもハイクコンテスト」のように、言葉の壁を越えて世界に広げていけたら——にぎやかな『まちのうた』を読みながら、今、そんなことを考えています。

こども本の森 中之島

The beacon of hope in the world

Tadao Ando
Architect

Haiku is a three-line poem that conveys the emotions of everyday life. Children from all over the world participate in this exciting language game in their native languages. I think it is a wonderful project filled with creativity. This time, the theme is "towns." A seven-year-old child in Sri Lanka depicts the hustle and bustle of a vibrant port city, an eleven-year-old child in Russia depicts the warmth of lights at night in one of the coldest cities in the world, and a twelve-year-old child in Romania depicts a world of fantasy set amidst a labyrinth of a medieval forest. All of them beautifully portray "their towns" as seen through their eyes in their own words and drawings. Each haiku depicts the scene and their emotions so vividly that I feel a fresh sensation within myself that "The planet we live on is so diverse and rich!" Just as I thought, children who are pure and honest are more creative than adults.

We are facing many complex and difficult challenges such as climate change, economic disparity, a food crisis, an energy crisis, a pandemic, and endless wars. On the other hand, continuous technological innovations have brought about rapid changes in society, and uncertainty and anxiety seem to pervade today's world.

Even under these circumstances, children never lose their sparkle. They are a beacon of hope in the world. To keep that light shining, we as adults must work hard to nurture children who will build the future. They possess that possibility in their innocent curiosity and inquisitiveness. We just need a place to accept it and nurture it.

After Andrew Carnegie made a fortune, he turned to philanthropy and helped build over 2,500 libraries around the world. Through my profession as an architect, I would also like to give back to society what it gave to me. With that in mind, I am promoting the Children's Book Forest Project of building and donating a library on land prepared by the city, collecting books, and operating through the people's support. It is a children's library that can be realized through public-private partnership. Three libraries have already been completed, starting with my home city Osaka, and four more are being planned in Japan and overseas. I would like to expand this project to the world beyond language barriers, just like the World Children's Haiku Contest. This is what came to my mind as I read "Impressions of Towns."

街の近くの
古い風車
春をぐるぐる

The old mill
Near the city
Churning springtime

Stari mlin
U blizini grada
Vrti proljeće

Franko Šćulac
Franko Sculac
age10
Croatia（クロアチア）

stari mlin
u blizini grada
vrti proljeće

From higher above
Overlooking the entire Taipei City
What a majestic scenery

居高臨下
俯瞰整座台北市
繁華盡收眼底

王 婉馨
Wan Wan-Xin
age12
Taiwan（台湾／台北）

見おろせば
広がる台北の街並み
すばらしい景色を目に焼きつける

Beautiful town
People live in harmony
Kuala Lumpur

Bandarku indah
Rakyat hidup harmoni
Kuala Lumpur

∎∎∎∎∎∎∎∎∎∎

Puteri Nurlyiana Binti Raduan
age12
Malaysia（マレーシア）

美しい街で
人々は仲良く暮らす
クアラルンプール

From the top of the city
I would like to glide away
On the wings of the wind

Z vrha mesta
Rada bi odplula stran
Na krilih vetra

∎∎∎∎∎∎∎∎∎∎

Auri Čučnik
age13
Slovenia（スロベニア）

街のてっぺんから
スーッと乗ってみたい
風の翼に

The wind blows hard here
Willis Tower stands so tall
Our Cubs play baseball

∎∎∎∎∎∎∎∎∎∎

Henry Muranaka
age 9
USA（米国／シカゴ）

ここは風が強い
ウィリス・タワーは高くそびえ
野球はぼくらのカブスだ

Little houses
With lots of greenery
And friends

Male hišice
Ter veliko zelenja
In prijateljev

Neža Sterle
age 7
Slovenia（スロベニア）

小<rt>ちい</rt>さなお家<rt>うち</rt>には
緑<rt>みどり</rt>がいっぱい
そして友<rt>とも</rt>だちも

The twin towers are spectacular
Go into the dragon tower then walk out from the tiger tower
The lotus is really beautiful

雙塔很ㄓㄨㄤ ˋ 觀
ㄉㄨㄥ ˊ 口進ㄏㄨˇ 口出
荷花ㄓㄣ 美麗

━━━━━━━━━━

蘇 怡蓁
Su Yi-Chen
age 8
Taiwan（台湾／高雄）

龍虎塔は堂々としているよ
入口は龍、出口は虎
蓮の花がきれい

Grapevine is peaceful
Everytime you walk in
You feel so much joy

━━━━━━━━━━

Victoria Garcia
age 8
USA（米国／ダラス）

グレイプバインは平和な街
来るたびに
いっぱい喜びを感じるの

Skyscrapers are standing
People and cars are rushing
A tree grows slowly

Wieżowce stoją
Ludzie i auta pędzą
Drzewo rośnie wolno

━━━━━━━━━━

Antonina Zakałużna
Antonina Zakaluzna
age 8
Poland（ポーランド）

高いビルが並び
人も車も忙しそう
木はゆっくり育つ

Wieżowce stoją
ludzie i auta pędzą
drzewo rośnie wolno

いくつも風車が
通りすぎる風に
回る回る

Windmills
With the passing air
Turn and turn

Molinos de viento
Con el aire al pasar
Giran y giran

Triana Fresco Retamosa
age 7
Spain （スペイン）

Molinos de viento
con el aire al pasar
giran y giran.

朝の煙
煙突を探して
路面電車が行く

Morning smoke
Scattered in search of a chimney
A lone tram wanders

Hommikune suits
Hajub korstent otsides
Eksleb üksik tramm

Marie Sarah Andresson
age 8
Estonia （エストニア）

見てるのは
野良猫たち
満月

I can see
The stray cats
Full moon

Виждам
Уличните котки
Пълна луна

Владина Тихолова
Vladina Tiholova
age15
Bulgaria （ブルガリア）

美しい上海港
大きな船が昼も夜も大忙し
未来は明るい

Shanghai Bay of beauty
Day and night ferries go busily
Hopes are more likely

美丽上海港
巨轮进出日夜忙
创造着希望

美丽上海港
巨轮进出日夜忙
创造着希望

城市

封 华
Feng Hua
age 8　China（中国／上海）

11

コンクリートジャングル
ビルの谷間でひと休み
お月さまがこんにちは

Living in concrete forest
Resting from work, sitting between buildings
The moonshine is greeting

อาศัยในป่าปูน
พักจากงานนั่งอยู่ซอกตึก
แสงจันทร์ลอดทักทาย

- - - - - - - - - -

เขมจิรา หอมรื่น
Keamjira Hormruen
age12
Thailand（タイ）

Above the gray
There is a blue heavenly sky
That reflects me

Sopra il grigio c'è
Un cielo blu celeste
Che mi riflette

- - - - - - - - - -

Chiara De Luca
age14
Italy（イタリア）

灰色の上の
天国みたいな青い空
私を映してる

The sun goes down
Leaving behind its light
Over my city

El sol se esconde
Dejando a ras su luz
Sobre mi ciudad

- - - - - - - - - -

Carlota Gómez Rebollo
age 8
Spain（スペイン）

日が沈み
光は残る
わたしの街

街の明かりの
シルエットの上に星が輝き
うるさくて元気な僕の街

Up above the city lights
Above the skyline, where the stars shine
My town's alive with noise

Khushal Sharma
age13
India（インド）

Up above the city lights.
above the skyline, where the stars shine.
My town's alive with noise.

大都市の夜
星はきらめきユラユラ
夢の中

Metropolitan night
Stars twinkle in the sky
Shining light over my dream

大都市的夜
星光闪烁在摇曳
漫游在梦里

樊 子钧
Fan Zijun
age 9
China（中国／上海）

朝日を浴びて
学校へゆっくり自転車をこぐ
ザーンダムの街中を抜けて

In the morning sun
He slowly cycles to his school
Through Zaandam Centre

In de morgenzon
Fietst hij langzaam naar zijn school
Door Zaandam Centrum

Enzo Winterink
age12
Netherlands（オランダ）

メロディーに乗せて
何百万もの世界を
大切な夢と一緒に

Stuck in melody
Through millions of worlds
With cherished dreams

Энэ сайхан хөгжимнөөс салж чадахгүй нь
Олон жилийн турш бичигдэж ирсэн энэ сайхан үгнүүд
Ар араасаа урссаар байна

■■■■■■■■■■

Баяртулга Саруул
Bayartulga Saruul
age11　Mongolia（モンゴル）

ビルに囲まれて
騒々しいのは群衆
ひとりぼっちの夜

Surrounded by the buildings
Noisy are the crowd
Sitting lonely at night

รายล้อมไปด้วยตึก
เสียงครึกครื้นไปด้วยผู้คน
นั่งเหงายามค่ำคืน

■■■■■■■■■■

วริศรา ว่านกระ
Warisara Wankra
age14　Thailand（タイ）

美しい街
にぎやかで忙しくて
私もそのひとり

Beautiful city
The hustle and bustle stand in rows
And I am in it

美丽的城市
繁华喧嚣排排立
而我在其中

■■■■■■■■■■

Wu Sixuan
age12
China（中国／天津）

14

We play and we share
We meet we greet and we care
Live in harmony

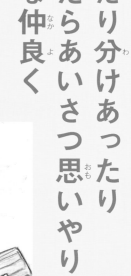

Ivanka Chantelle Wimalarathne
age 8
Singapore（シンガポール）

遊んだり分けあったり
会ったらあいさつ思いやり
みんな仲良く

15

この建物から
目ざめる街
すべてが生きかえる

Above this buiding
The city wakes up
And everything comes back to life

Sur cet immeuble
La ville se réveille
Et tout reprend vie

■■■■■■■■■■

Kuhn Anaëlle
age11
France（フランス）

シンガポール・フライヤー
かっこいい大観覧車
夢は広がるどこまでも

The Singapore Flyer
A picturesque view of the Singapore Flyer
Where dreams do not end

■■■■■■■■■■

Sim Jia Qi Jesse Christelle
age 8
Singapore（シンガポール）

夜の都会
輝く星と白い月
わぁ、なんてきれい！

Cities of nightfall
Shiny stars and clear white moon
Oh, how beautiful！

城市的夜晚
閃亮的星與皓月
嘩！多麼美麗！

陳 力予
Chan Nick Yu
age10
China（中国／香港）

Concrete jungle
A hiding place behind blocks of flats
This is my home！

Betonska džungla
Skrivališča za bloki
Tukaj sem doma！

Anadin Zahirović
age15
Slovenia（スロベニア）

コンクリートジャングル
集合住宅の裏に隠れて
ここが僕の家！

Night in a little mountain town
On the sleeping cottages
The moon shines

Планинско градче
В къщички заспали
Свети луната

Десислава Калоферова
Desislava Kaloferova
age 6
Bulgaria（ブルガリア）

やまのちいさなまち
よるにねむるいえいえを
つきがてらす

В ДЕЛНИЦИ, ПРАЗНИЦИ
ТЕЧЕ ЖИВОТЪТ
ОБИЧАМ ТЕ, МОЙ ГРАД !

平日も休日も
人生は流れる
大好き、わたしの街！

On weekdays and holidays
Life flows
I love you, my town!

В делници, празници
Тече животът
Обичам те, мой град !

Петя Димитрова
Petya Dimitrova
age11
Bulgaria（ブルガリア）

The sun is rising
Over the city
The day starts so well

Die sonne geht auf
Über der stadt. Das ist schön
Der tag fängt gut an

Nina Fendel
age12
Germany（ドイツ）

日が昇ってくる
街の上に
いい一日の始まり

Die Sonne geht auf
über der Stadt. Das ist sch
Der Tag fängt gut an.

Birds sing on the trees
Crowds at the farmers market
Feeling the wind blow

Norah Kennedy
age 8
Canada（カナダ）

木で鳥が歌い
にぎわうファーマーズマーケット
風を感じるよ

19

街はきれい
きれいな空気と木々
そしてきれいな道

City is a beautiful place
The clean air and beautiful trees
And beautiful streets

Cidade é um lugar lindo
O ar puro e árvores lindas
E estradas lindas

Tamires Da Graça Chaile
age11
Mozambique（モザンビーク）

The city
Is growing as bamboo
We're sleeping in clouds . . .

Город
Растёт как бамбук
Спим в облаках...

街は竹みたいに
まっすぐ伸びて
ぼくらは雲の中で眠る

Анатолий Петухов
Anatoliy Petukhov
age11
Russia（ロシア）

真っ暗な街
ワクワクして目を開けると
美しい夜

A pitch-dark city
I opened my eyes with joy
Appreciating the beauty of the night

漆黑的城市
欣欣然睜開了眼
讀夜的美麗

■■■■■■■■■■

林 亮宇
Lin Liang-Yu
age12
Taiwan（台湾／高雄）

漆黑的城市
欣欣然睜開了眼
讀夜的美麗

The beauty of the mountains
Hidden by buildings
What a pleasant sight

La beauté des monts
Cachés par les bâtiments
Quelle vue agréable

■■■■■■■■■■

Desagher Eloïme
age10
France（フランス）

山の美しさは
ビルに隠れても
楽しい景色

窓の下に
見える四角い星々
ついたり消えたり

Under my window
I see square stars
They turn on and off

Sob minha janela
Enxergo estrelas quadradas
Ligam e desligam

Ana Luiza Pacheco Muracca Yoshinaga
age11
Brazil（ブラジル）

SOB MINHA JANELA
ENXERGO ESTRELAS QUADRADAS
LIGAM E DESLIGAM

僕の願い
きれいな街に
緑豊かな街に

My wish
May the city be clean
In greenery

मेरो चाहना
सफा सहरहोस्,
हरियालीमा

सन्जल श्रेष्ठ
Sanjal Shrestha
age14
Nepal（ネパール）

Twinkle twinkle neon lights shine
Fireworks in Disneyland sparkle in the sky
A glaring city saying hi

霓虹灯闪烁
迪士尼里升烟火
城市开花朵

キラキラ光るネオン
空にディズニーランドの花火
きらめく街からこんにちは

胡 以信
Hu Yixin
age 9
China（中国／上海）

22

わたしの街は忙しい
でも幸せがいっぱい
そして、とってもきれい

My town is busy
But full of happy
And looks so pretty

■■■■■■■■■■

Thanumi De Silva
age 7
Sri Lanka（スリランカ）

Roaring Singapore
Hustling, burstling, full of life
Never ending lights

■■■■■■■■■■

Vivienne Crystalynne Elle Lie
age10
Singapore（シンガポール）

にぎやかなシンガポール
押しあいへしあい元気いっぱい
いつまでも輝きつづける

23

There is an old bridge in the town
A good place for walking and fishing
The sea view is really beautiful

城裡有老橋
散步釣魚好地方
海景真是美

郭 瀚天
Kuo Han-Tian
age11
Taiwan（台湾／高雄）

街にある古い橋
散歩や釣りの穴場
海の景色が本当に美しい

幸せな世界
手の中にすっぽり
わたしの街

My town
I have held
The happy world

मेरो सहर
पक्डेर राखेको छु
सुखी संसार

रिया पोखरेल
Riya Pokharel
age11
Nepal（ネパール）

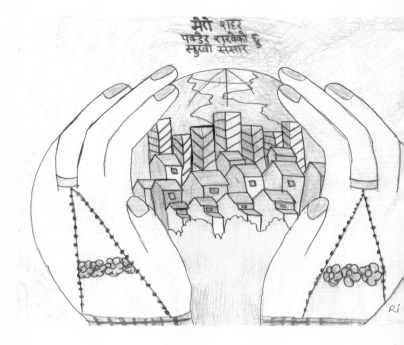

Designs fill the air
Inspirations everywhere
It's cold beware

Corey Bicknell
age10
USA（米国／ボストン）

寒いから気をつけて
ひらめきはどこにでも
デザインがいっぱい

The Aegean Sea
In love with
The brand new seagull

Ege Denizi
Çiçeği burnundaki
Martıya aşık

Elif Topaç
Elif Topac
age13
Turkey（トルコ）

恋愛中
若いカモメに
エーゲ海

星光和灯光
城市夜色多迷离
犹如在梦里

With the stars and lights
The city night is blurred
As if in a dream

星光和灯光
城市夜色多迷离
犹如在梦里

■■■■■■■■■

张 瑞文
Zhang Xiwen
age 8
China（中国／上海）

星と明かりで
にじんだような街の夜
夢の中みたい

Tall tower
A very busy city
A place to find money

Menara tinggi
Sibuk sungguh di bandar
Lubuk rezeki

■■■■■■■■■

Mieya Qhumairah Binti Mohd Nudzul Hakim
age12
Malaysia（マレーシア）

高層タワー
とても忙しい街
お金の集まるところ

Moonlight
Puts houses to sleep
Only silence bubbles

Mėnulio šviesa
Užmigdo miesto namus
Knibžda tik tyla

■■■■■■■■■

Augustė Jokšaitė
Auguste Joksaite
age12
Lithuania（リトアニア）

月光が
家々を眠らせ
静けさがあふれる

別々の街に住み
でも、同じ
うれしい気持ち

Living in two different cities
But the same
Happy feeling

Хоёр өөр
Хотод байлаа ч
Аз жаргалыг мэдрэнэ

Майнтуяа Мөнхтуяа
Maintuya Munkhtuya
age11
Mongolia（モンゴル）

何百万人もの
巨大都市
ひとりで歩く

Giant cities
With millions of people
Walking solitarily

Cidades gigantes
Com milhões de pessoas
Andando solitárias

Jane Aparecida Nunes Dranski
age11
Brazil（ブラジル）

大都会の小さな家
お昼寝している
雨の日

A small house
In a big city is taking a nap
On a rainy day

Majhna hiša v
Velikem mestu drema
Na deževni dan

Hana Kosmač
age12
Slovenia（スロベニア）

水鏡
青い川面に
映る家並み

Mirroring
In the blue river reflection
The houses

Espelhando-se
No rio azul reflexo
Do casario

Rita Pires Ferreira
age15
Portugal（ポルトガル）

espelhando-se
no rio azul reflexo
do casario

Beautiful majestic
Historical city
Our heritage

Tersergam megah
Bandar bersejarahku
Warisan kita

Nur Nashrullah Bin Nur Azlin
age10
Malaysia（マレーシア）

立派で美しい
歴史的な街並み
ぼくたちの遺産

Just like a flying eagle
Soring higher in the sky
Can you see me？

我像一隻鷹
翱翔在城市上空
你看到了嗎？

郭 清子
Guo Cing-Tzu
age10
Taiwan（台湾／台北）

わたしは鷹になって
街の空高く舞いあがる
わたしが見える？

ホノルルの太陽
楽しい街に降りそそぐ
空はいつもカラフル

The Sun in Honolulu
Shines through the happy town
And always makes the skies colorful

■■■■■■■■■■

Lino Yamamoto
age11
USA（米国／ハワイ）

Las flores rojas
las calles coloridas
México lindo

赤い花
色とりどりの街
華やかなメキシコ

The red flowers
The colorful streets
Beautiful Mexico

Las flores rojas
Las calles coloridas
México lindo

Daniela Vargas Pérez
age10
Mexico（メキシコ）

霧の窓の向こうに
でっかいエレベーター塔
家に帰る目印だ

Out of the foggy window
The gargantuan lift tower
Guiding us home again

Samuel Debenham
age10
UK（英国）

街は変わり
交わる命
川は流れる

The city changes
Lives intersect
The river runs

A cidade muda
As vidas cruzam-se
O rio corre

Mariana Filipa Marques Fernandes
age14
Portugal（ポルトガル）

平和でやさしい詩のように
やわらかな月光が屋根に
都会の静かな夜

Silent city night
Silk moonlight fallen on the roof
Like a peaceful and lovely poetry

城市寧靜的夜
柔和月光灑落屋頂啊
平靜美麗的詩意

■■■■■■■■■■

李 幸薰
Lee Hsin-Shun
age10
Taiwan（台湾／台北）

僕らの願い
文化的な街カトマンズ

Our wish
In Kathmandu
Cultural town

काठमाण्डौमा
सांस्कृतिक शहर
तम्रो रहर

■■■■■■■■■■

सुरज सिङ ठकुरी
Suraj Singh Thakuri
age14
Nepal（ネパール）

街灯の下に立つ
雨粒に囲まれ
塔の庭で

In the garden of towers
Among the droplets of water
To stand under the lamp

W ogrodzie wież
Wśród drobnych kropli wody
Stać pod lampą

■■■■■■■■■■

Lena Bernatek
age14
Poland（ポーランド）

街（まち）
ゆっくりと変（か）わりゆく
その物語（ものがたり）

The town
Its stories
Slowly change

Градът
Бавно историите
Се променят

Любомира Симеонова
Lyubomira Simeonova
age14
Bulgaria（ブルガリア）

Digitalization presents prosperity
Preserving environment fosters growth
Vitality of the city

數碼展繁華
環境保育助發展
都會顯活力

デジタル化（か）は繁栄（はんえい）の印（しるし）
発展（はってん）のための環境（かんきょう）保全（ほぜん）
都市（とし）の活力（かつりょく）

曾 樂淘
Tsang Lok Tao
age11
China（中国／香港）

Mother Nepal
Blooming as flower
Our city

नेपाल आमा
फूल भैं फूलेकी छिन्
हाम्रो शहर

母（はは）なるネパール
花（はな）のように咲（さ）きほこる
私（わたし）たちの街（まち）

रेखा गिरी
Rekha Giri
age14
Nepal（ネパール）

放課後
公園の栗を
ポケットにいっぱい

Classes are over
Chestnuts in the city park
Filled in my pockets

Pamokos baigės
Miesto parke kaštonai
Pilnos kišenės

Alesandra Kononenko
age10　Lithuania（リトアニア）

It's a beautiful, modern, living, spring city.

うつくしき
いのちきらめく
はるのまち

It's a beautiful
Modern living
Spring city

Хаврын хот
Сэтгэл сэргэм
Үзэсгэлэнтэй

Цогтбаяр Ариунцэцэг
Tsogtbayar Ariuntsetseg
age12
Mongolia（モンゴル）

美しき
生命きらめく
春の街

早すぎる時の流れ
立ちどまって子どもたちと一緒にワクワクと世界を眺められる人はいるかしら?
人生は忙しく、とても短い

Time past by so fast
Who can stop to watch this world curiously with children
Life is too short yet too busy

時間啊隨著日子飛逝
有誰能和孩子停下腳步好奇地看世界呢
一生的時間很少所以大家都很忙碌

Zhang Yu-Han
age13
Taiwan（台湾／台北）

Opened balcony
I'm watering the city garden
It's finally summer

Balkon otwarty
Podlewam miejski ogród
W końcu lato

■■■■■■■■■■

Alicja Boczoń
Alicia Boczon
age13
Poland（ポーランド）

開けはなたれたバルコニー
街の庭に水やりをする
いよいよ夏だ

Balkon otwarty
podlewam miejski ogród
w końcu lato!

As the flowering trees bloom
The town regains color and so do
The people living within it

■■■■■■■■■■

Suhasini Sen
age11
India（インド）

木々に花が咲いて
街に色がもどる
そこに住むみんなにも

Golden shining sun
Therapeutic experience
Relaxing evening

■■■■■■■■■■

Leroy Ho Xian Yang
age 9
Singapore（シンガポール）

金色に輝くお日さま
やさしくいやしてくれる
のんびりする夕べ

Spring night
The song of the crickets
In the park

Noche de primavera
El canto de los grillos
En el parque

■■■■■■■■■■

Alejandro Gómez Pletea
age 7
Spain（スペイン）

春の夜
コオロギの歌
公園に

Noche de primavera
el canto de los grillos
en el parque.

36

木々の歌
青葉(あおば)かがやく
バルセロナ

Songs of the trees
Green leaves shining
Barcelona

■■■■■■■■■

亀川 南帆
Naho Kamegawa
age12
Japan（日本）

Boston in summer
People would go to the beach
They have fun all day!

▪▪▪▪▪▪▪▪▪▪

Jessica Vanegas
age11
USA（米国／ボストン）

ボストンの夏
みんなビーチに行って
一日中楽しむ！

The ocean, so loud
Hearing all the waves crashing
With sand in my toes

▪▪▪▪▪▪▪▪▪▪

Landen Victoria Y. Devera
age13
USA（米国／グアム）

海、ものすごい音
波がくだけるのを聞いてる
足の指に砂をつけて

厳かな日の出
幸先のよい仕事はじめ
希望ある未来へ

Glorious sunrise
People work for a head start
With hopeful futures

■■■■■■■■■■

Jianing Wu
age14
Indonesia（インドネシア）

39

City in white
It's a pity for the pine
It will be all alone

Città in bianco
Peccato per il pino
Sarà da solo

■■■■■■■■■■

Marco Muollo
age10
Italy（イタリア）

白い街
松はかわいそうに
ひとりぼっちになりそう

The night in Boston
The wind comes, the city in peace
The wind starts to blow

■■■■■■■■■■

Joanna Chen
age10
USA（米国／ボストン）

ボストンの夜
静かな街に風が来て
吹きはじめる

Sometimes I feel
When I close my eyes I hear
The rush of water in the city

Vahel tunnen, et
Kui silmad sulen, kuulen
Veekohinat linnas

━━━━━━━━━━

Ketlin Samblik
age11
Estonia（エストニア）

ときどき感じるの
目を閉じると聞こえてくる
街の中の水の音

In the beautiful city
A train passes, a leaf flies
The sun rises

Dans la belle ville
Un train passe, une feuille vole
Le soleil se lève

━━━━━━━━━━

Lopez Antoine
age11
France（フランス）

美しい街に
電車が走り、葉っぱが舞う
日が昇る

家々をおおう
深く積もった雪
サンクトペテルブルク

Houses are covered
In a layer of thick snow
In St. Petersburg

■■■■■■■■■■

Mariam Hasan
age11
Norway/Sweden（ノルウェー／スウェーデン）

A turtle
With her feathery socks
Under the sand

Bir kaplumbağa
Tüylü çoraplarıyla
Kumun altında

一匹のカメ
毛糸の靴下はいて
砂の中で冬眠中

Melis Tapanoğlu
Melis Tapanoglu
age11
Turkey（トルコ）

Car window
A lychee seller tells
It is early summer

車窓から
初夏の知らせの
ライチ売り

橋本 心響
Kokona Hashimoto
age15
Japan（日本）

Dew is still on the branches
The street is still quietly asleep
People are doing excercise

Sương còn đọng trên cành
Phố xá còn im lìm giấc ngủ
Người đã tập thể thao

枝には朝露
街はまだ眠っている
体操する人々

Nguyễn Hoàng Quyên
Nguyen Hoang Quyen
age 9
Vietnam（ベトナム）

すごい球場だ
選手たちは大喜び
凍るほど寒い

An amazing place
Our sports teams are very graced
Very icy-cold

Brendan Skehill
age11
USA（米国／ボストン）

桜の花
暗い夜空には星
東京の春

Cherry blossoms
Dark and starry nights
Spring in Tokyo

Fleurs de cerisiers
Nuits sombres et étoilées
Printemps à Tokyo

Emeriault Apolline
age11
France（フランス）

Red dawn sky
Shadows give pictures of
The city of Paris

∎∎∎∎∎∎∎∎

中山 七海
Nanami Nakayama
age12
Japan（日本）

朝焼けで
かげ絵が創る
パリのまち

朝焼けで
かげ絵が創る
パリのまち

街をおおう雨雲
紙の舟で洪水をわたる
ひとりの子

Rainclouds over town
Waiting to ride the flood with paper boat
A child

Osu mununkum gu kurow no so

Abofra bi

A wɔretwɛn sɛ wɔde krataa hyɛmma bɛtra nsuyiri no so

∎∎∎∎∎∎∎∎

Mensah Miranda
age15
Ghana（ガーナ）

On light cables
The owl is perched
Nightfall in the city

Nos fios de luz
Pousa a coruja
Anoitece na cidade

電
線
に
梟
が
止
ま
っ
て
街
は
夕
暮
れ

Ana Clara Oliveira Santos
age10
Brazil（ブラジル）

Storm strikes the town
Hot chestnuts in his hand
A friend awaits

Bura gura grad
Vrući kesten u ruci
Prijatelj čeka

嵐
が
街
を
襲
う
熱
々
の
栗
を
手
に
友
が
待
っ
て
い
る

Vibor Drenjak
age14
Croatia（クロアチア）

家々は人々のように
凍りつく寒さの中で身を寄せあう
それでみんなあたたかい

Houses like people
Snuggle to each other in the cold
And all of us feel warm

Дома, как люди
Жмутся к друг другу в мороз
И нам всем тепло

■■■■■■■■■

Михаил Маскаев
Mikhail Maskaev
age11
Russia（ロシア）

ДОМА, КАК ЛЮДИ
ЖМУТСЯ К ДРУГУ Е
И НАМ ВСЕМ ТЕПЛО

夕立の
音だけひびく
アーケード

Only the sound of
An evening shower
Arcade

■■■■■■■■■

坂元 遙
Haruka Sakamoto
age 8
Japan（日本）

風が冷たい
絡みあったバラの
根っこはひとつ

The wind is cold
I see all roses entwined
Roots together as one

■■■■■■■■■■

Isla Lucas
age 9
USA（米国／サンフランシスコ）

To the cherry-blossom viewing
I can walk
From my house

■■■■■■■■■■

藤井 湊太
Sota Fujii
age 6
Japan（日本）

おはなみへ
ぼくのいえから
あるいてく

大きな街
小さな野良猫
雪に隠れて

Big city
Little homeless kitten
Hiding in snow

Didžiulis miestas
Mažas benamis kačiukas
Slapstosi sniege

■■■■■■■■■■

Arnita Jokimaitytė
Arnita Jokimaityte
age11
Lithuania（リトアニア）

Didžiulis miestas
mažas benamis kačiukas
slapstosi sniege

It rains a lot
A grandmother on crutches
Crosses the street

Llueve mucho
Una abuela con muletas
Cruza la calle

■■■■■■■■■■

Leonor Jiménez Guzmán
age13
Spain（スペイン）

降りつづく雨
松葉杖のおばあさんが
道をわたる

49

秋の空
朝九時の
車両点検

Nine in the morning
Vehicle inspection
Autumn sky

川端 泰寛
Yasuhiro Kawabata
age 9
Japan （日本）

In the city port
The cranes are lifting
The morning fog

U gradskoj luci
Dizalice podižu
Jutarnju maglu

朝の霧
街の港で
クレーンが持ちあげる

Zlata Vrtodušić
Zlata Vrtodusic
age13
Croatia （クロアチア）

On a city bus
A butterfly on the window
Going together

Miesto autobuse
Drugelis prie lango
Važiuojame kartu

Lėja Adomavičiūtė
Leja Adomaviciute
age12
Lithuania （リトアニア）

市バスの
窓に蝶
一緒に乗ってる

静かな街
秋の夜のコオロギ
眠りを誘う

The city is quiet
Crickets sing softly at autumn night
Hypnotise to sleep

城市静悄悄
秋夜蟋蟀轻声唱
催眠入梦乡

■■■■■■■■■■

江 宸喧
Jiang Chenxuan
age10
China（中国／上海）

Olive tree
Greeting the sun
In my little garden

Zeytin ağacı
Selamlıyor güneşi
Küçük bahçemde

■■■■■■■■■■

Adnan Aras Özyürekoğlu
Adnan Aras Ozyurekoglu
age10
Turkey（トルコ）

オリーブの木が
太陽にこんにちは
小さなぼくの庭から

どこまでも
登れる気がする
夏の朝

Endlessly
I feel I can go up the stairs
Summer morning

■ ■ ■ ■ ■ ■ ■ ■ ■

島津 美耶
Miya Shimazu
age15
Japan（日本）

ど"こまでも
登れる気がする
夏の朝

In my city
I like to enjoy
The sun and the flowers

Na minha cidade
Eu gosto de apreciar
O sol e as flores

■ ■ ■ ■ ■ ■ ■ ■ ■

Leonor Carvalho Henriques
age11
Portugal（ポルトガル）

わたしの街
楽しんでいるわ
太陽と花を

The setting sun
Is turning the skyscrapers
Golden yellow

Sonce zahaja
Stolpnice postajajo
Zlatorumene

■ ■ ■ ■ ■ ■ ■ ■ ■

Tinkara Tušar
age14
Slovenia（スロベニア）

沈む夕日
高層ビル群を
黄金に染めて

太陽はとても明るい
太陽はものすごく熱い
太陽は喜びを届ける

The sun is so bright
The sun is extremely hot
The sun brings me joy

▪▪▪▪▪▪▪▪▪▪▪

Kayla McIntosh
age11
USA（米国／グアム）

53

Chestnuts
Waiting for us
On Granny's stove

Bekliyor bizi
Anneanne sobası
Kestaneleri

Nevra Tekçe
Nevra Tekce
age 7
Turkey （トルコ）

わたしたちを待っているよ
おばあちゃんのストーブの上
熱々の栗たちが

Summer town aglow
Sunshine gives warm hugs around
Thrusting off the shadows

Lydia Scott
age 9
UK （英国）

輝く夏の街
日光があたたかく抱きしめて
影を追いはらう

にぎやかな街の
夜空の花火、きれいなドレスみたい
小さな幸せを運んでくれる

Crowded town
Fireworks illuminate the dark sky
Delivering the happiness

擁擠的城市
煙花帶來美衣裳
傳送小幸福

林 姵辰
Lin Nina
age 9
Taiwan（台湾／台北）

Squall
Stops the time
At once

スコールで
時間が止まる
いっせいに

中村 柚月
Yuzuki Nakamura
age 9
Japan（日本）

In hot summer days
The gentle breeze brushed through the blue dyed cloth
The elegance of the old days reappeared

炎熱的夏日
微風輕拂藍染布
重現舊風華

- - - - - - - - -

陳 可芯
Chen Cecilia
age 9
Taiwan（台湾／高雄）

暑い夏の日
そよ風が藍染を揺らし
美しい昔がよみがえる

A rainy evening
The traffic light keeps watching
With changing light

En tardía lluvia
El semáforo vigila
Con luz cambiante

- - - - - - - - - -

Thiago Mateo Mejía Clemente
age 5
Mexico（メキシコ）

あめのゆうがた
しんごうがみまもってる
いろをかえながら

首都は
輝くリスボン
ベレンのエッグタルト

The capital is
Luminous Lisbon
Egg tarts of Belém

É a capital
Lisboa luminosa
Pastéis de Belém

Dânia Marques
age 9
Portugal（ポルトガル）

É a capi
Lisboa lum
Pastéis de

かけ声と
色がはじける
マーケット

Shouts and
Colors popping
At the market

■■■■■■■■■

宮澤 慶之
Yoshiyuki Miyazawa
age 9
Japan（日本）

かけ声と
色がはじける
マーケット

にぎやかな街の音
朝から晩までずっと続く
あっちにもこっちにも人

The noise of the city
From morning till evening for years
People are here and there

Хотын чимээ шуугиан
Хэдэн жил, өглөө орой
Энд тэндгүй хүмүүс

■■■■■■■■

Цэцэгмаа Энхлэн
Tsetsegmaa Enkhlen
age13
Mongolia（モンゴル）

朝
街に目ざめると
愛がいっぱい

In the morning
Wake up in the city
Full of love

Logo de manhã
Acordo na cidade
Cheia de amor

■■■■■■■

Margarida Isabel Conde Guilherme
age10
Portugal（ポルトガル）

すべてある
全部全部全部全部全部全部全部全部全部
思いつくすべて

Everything is there
All all all all all all all
The thought of everything

Kõik on olemas
Kõik kõik kõik kõik kõik kõik kõik
Mõtteummik kõik

■ ■ ■ ■ ■ ■ ■ ■ ■ ■

Mia Dolores Pavelson
age14
Estonia（エストニア）

ぼくの街は船
さあ、出港
果てしない海へ

My city is a ship
Setting sail
For the endless sea

Moj grad je brod
Koji plovi
U beskrajno more

■ ■ ■ ■ ■ ■ ■ ■ ■ ■

Niko Miknić
Niko Miknic
age11
Croatia（クロアチア）

moj grad je brod
koji plovi
u beskrajno more

ディンドンディンドンと駅のメロディー
地下鉄の扉が閉まる
にぎやかさはどこにいったの

Ding dong ding dong song
The underground is closing
Where is the hustle and bustle

叮咚叮咚歌
地铁就要关门了
熙熙攘攘呢

――――――――

曽 林烁
Zeng Linshuo
age 9
China（中国／広州）

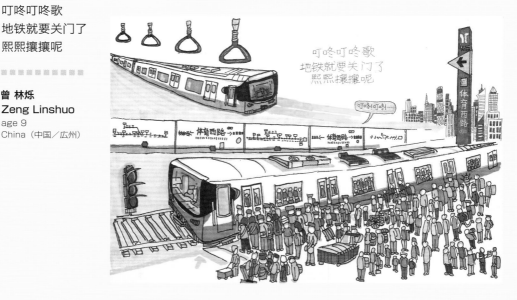

A lonely heart
Wandering on the pavement
Looking for itself

Vieniša širdis
Klaidžiojanti šaligatviu
Ieškanti savęs

さびしい心
歩道にさまよう
自らを探して

Patricija Danytė
Patricija Danyte
age12
Lithuania（リトアニア）

At the city park
Children with balloons
Adults on cellphones

No parque da cidade
Crianças com balão
Adultos no celular

街の公園に
風船を持つ子ども
スマホに夢中な大人

――――――――

Nicole Franciele Pedrozo Oliveira
age14
Brazil（ブラジル）

やせたお母さん
路上で物売りに忙しい
家族のために

My poor skinny mom
She is busy with street vendor
Making a living on the streets

Thương lắm tấm thân gầy
Mẹ tảo tần với gánh hàng rong
Mưu sinh khắp phố phường

∎∎∎∎∎∎∎∎∎∎

Lê Phương Tú
Le Phuong Tu
age13
Vietnam（ベトナム）

The crowded city
The children escape
In old fairy tales

Oraşul aglomerat
Copiii evadează
În vechi basme

Butnărescu Lasmina
age12
Romania（ルーマニア）

ゴチャゴチャした街
子どもたちが逃げこむ
古いおとぎ話

crowded city—
the children escape
in old fairy tales

空が漏って
通りに水たまり
そして雷が鳴りひびく

The sky is leaking
As my street becomes puddles
And thunder echoes

Lilah Thomas
age12
Canada（カナダ）

天井を見た
クモの巣の模様で
眠りに落ちた

I looked at the ceiling
A spider in its web
I fell asleep

Tavana baktım
Bir örümcek ağında
Uykuya daldım

Defne Tuğba Avcı
Defne Tugba Avci
age 8
Turkey（トルコ）

うっとりするメロディー
はっきりつよくみみにとどく
まちにあふれるたのしいうたごえ

Beautiful
As sweet
Joyful songs fill the streets

娓娓动听
洋洋盈耳
欢乐歌声满街区

■■■■■■■■■

Gu Manqi
age 6
China（中国／大連）

娓娓动听
洋洋盈耳
欢乐歌声满街区

よるのおうちは
みんなでおはなししてるのかな
でもだれにもきこえないね

Houses together at night
Maybe talking but
No one can hear them

Majad öösel koos
Võibolla räägivad kuid
Keegi ei kuule neid

■■■■■■■■■

Lille Ly Sepp
age 6
Estonia（エストニア）

ガヤガヤとにぎやかな街
あたたかい街灯の光に包まれて
なぐさめられる空っぽの心

Bustling lively town
Wrapped in warm glow of street lights
Soothes my empty heart

■■■■■■■■■

Sofya Abdul Aziz
age12
Singapore（シンガポール）

Night of light
A thousand sounds in the city
And a thousand emptiness

Notti di luce
Mille suoni in città
E mille vuoti

■■■■■■■■■■

Malak Zehni
age15
Italy（イタリア）

光の夜
街に千の音
そして千の虚しさ

COVID attacked our town
Mom warmly embraced me
Looking at Dad's ashes

โควิดบุกเข้าเมือง
แม่โอบไหล่ฉันอย่างอบอุ่น
มองกระดูกของพ่อ

■■■■■■■■■■

มนตรี นันทา
Montree Nanta
age12
Thailand（タイ）

コロナが街を襲い
お母さんが僕をやさしく抱きしめた
お父さんの遺灰を見つめて

Dans la ville noire
Un renard et ses petits
Rentrent chez eux

Juliette

In the dark city
A fox and her babies
Go back home

Dans la ville noire
Un renard et ses petits
Rentrent chez eux

■■■■■■■■■■

Juliette Van Raepenbusch
age 8
Belgium（ベルギー）

暗い街
狐の親子が
お家に帰る

In this cusp of the world
Where rain cascades, where we grow
And where love flourishes

■■■■■■■■■■

Asha Parmar
age12
Canada（カナダ）

雨が降りそそぎ、私たちが成長する
この世界の先端は
愛が栄えるところ

In this cusp of the world
Where rain cascades, Where We grow
And where love flourishes

People in the city
An awful lot of people
And I don't stand out

Mensen in de stad
Verschrikkelijk veel mensen
En ik val niet op

■■■■■■■■■■

Pien Elfrink
age11
Netherlands（オランダ）

街の人たち
ものすごい数の人たち
紛れてしまうわたし

Skipping home from school
Red light flashes, bus splashes
Puddle in my shoes

■■■■■■■■■■

Amelia Kan
age 8
UK（英国）

学校からスキップで帰る
赤信号が点滅、バスが水をはねる
わたしのくつはずぶ濡れ

Here is a sea turtle
Living under deep blue sea
Protecting our cherish home

有一隻烏龜
住在藍藍的大海
守護我們家

■■■■■■■■■■

王 信喆
Wang Hsin-Che
age 5
Taiwan（台湾／台北）

うみがめがいるよ
あおいあおいうみにすんで
ぼくらのいえをまもっているよ

街の市場
歌で人形に生命を吹きこみ
精霊をたたえる売り子

Town market
Singing life into her dolls
A vendor serves her spirit

Kurow no mu gua so
Adetɔnfo bi som ne ahonhom
Ɔtu nkwa dwom gu ne abaduaba mu

Fuseini Samira
age15
Ghana（ガーナ）

It got me again . . .
The old passion for adventures
Strive new, freedom and love

Завладя ме пак
Онази стара страст приключенска
Устрем нов, свобода и любов

またつかまった
冒険への古い情熱
新しい自由と愛を求めて

Стела Иванова
Stela Ivanova
age14
Bulgaria（ブルガリア）

It is lighting
The light earth in
Sunny world

Энэ хот гэрэлтэж байна
Гэрэлт дэлхий
Хамгийн үзэсгэлэнтэй

街が光ってる
光る世界が
一番きれい

Батзориг Мичидмаа
Batzorig Michidmaa
age 7
Mongolia（モンゴル）

Chugga chugga choo choo
McDonald's doorbell "ding dong" sounds like a happy song
It's the symphony of the town

ㄉ ㄤ ㄉ ㄤ ㄐ ㄧ ㄐ ㄧ ㄑ ㄧ

ㄅ ㄧˊ ㄉ ㄨ ㄥ ㄇ ㄞ ˋ ㄉ ㄤ ㄠˊ ㄎ ㄨ ㄞˋ ㄌ ㄜˋ ㄙ ㄨ ㄥˋ

ㄔ ㄥˊ ㄓ ㄣˋ ㄐ ㄧ ㄠˇ ㄒ ㄧ ㄤˇ ㄑ ㄩˇ

荘 睿穎
Chuang Jui-Ying
age 7
Taiwan（台湾／高雄）

Chasing a chicken
Is very fun but tiring
At the slopes near my house

Liew Wen Xin
age13
Singapore（シンガポール）

鶏と追いかけっこ
楽しいけれど、ちょっと疲れる
家の前の坂

シュッシュッ ポッポー
「ピンポーン」マクドナルドのドアベル楽しい
みんな街の歌

No discrimination is anywhere
No judging by appearance
Everyone is treated equally

■■■■■■■■■■

Zoey Ng
age 9
USA（米国／サンフランシスコ）

どこにも差別はない
見かけで決めつけない
みんな平等

ラマダン明けが近い
街は静かに
休息のひととき

Approaching to Eid
Lost occupants in the city
Time to rest

Menjelang raya
Penghuni bandar hilang
Masa berehat

■■■■■■■■■■

Nurul Husna Binti Mohd Sukri
age13
Malaysia（マレーシア）

Menjelang raya
Penghuni bandar hilang
masa berehat

光、音、ゴチャゴチャ
街をあちこち歩く
なんてちっぽけな僕

Lights noise and chaos
Wandering through the city
See how small I am

■■■■■■■■■■

Hector Stroud Arzua
age12
UK（英国）

かも２ひき
パンやの前を
とおってる

Two ducks
Passing
In front of a bakery

■■■■■■■■■■

王 媛一
Wang Yuanyi
age 7
Japan（日本）

夜が来て
わたしの思いは灯りみたいに
眠らない

Night is falling
My thoughts like light
No sleep

Öö on käes
Mu mõtted nagu valgus
Ei maga

Kira Mihhailova
Kira Mikhaylova
age10
Estonia（エストニア）

丘の上から
贖罪のキリストが見守る
洪水の街

From the top of the hill
Christ the redeemer observes
The flooded city

Do alto do morro
Cristo redentor observa
A cidade inundada

Tainná Vitor Dos Santos
age15
Brazil（ブラジル）

見て、街があるよ
でもぼくたちは行けない
道は知っている

Look here is a city
But we can't go there
I know the way

Kijk hier is een stad
Maar we kunnen er niet heen
Ik weet de weg wel

Jonas Giling
age 7
Netherlands（オランダ）

Convenient city
Accessible to all necessities
Show city our love

城市真方便
衣食住行樣樣齊
齊來愛護它

便利な街
なんでも手に入る
街を大切にしよう

梁 匡澄
Leung Hong Ching
age 9
China（中国／香港）

Various cities all over the world
Uncountable colors, forms, voices
Yet love is all around us

Տարբեր քաղաքներ
Անթիվ գույներ ձևեր ձայներ
Բայց ամենուր սեր

Դավիթ Պողիկյան
David Poghikyan
age11
Armenia（アルメニア）

世界中の街
数えきれない色と形と声
でも愛に包まれて

My city falls asleep
Wrapped in smog
Like a big white cat

Засыпает мой город
В смог завернувшись
Как большой белый кот

Арсений Заболотной
Arseny Zabolotny
age13
Estonia（エストニア）

僕の街は眠りにつく
大きな白猫みたいな
スモッグに包まれて

In Chinatown Point
Filled up with different races
Chatting happily

Tasha Fu Xuan En
age10
Singapore（シンガポール）

チャイナタウン・ポイント
いろんな人が集まって
楽しくおしゃべり

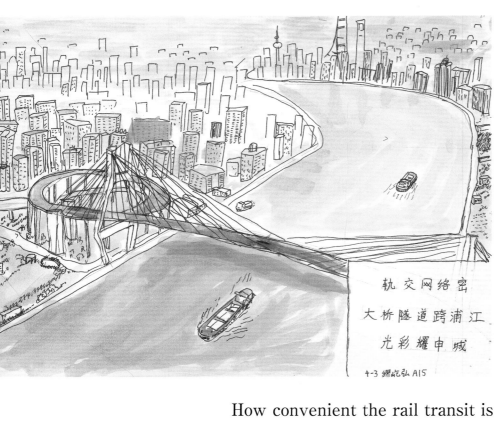

鉄道はとても便利
黄浦江の両岸を橋とトンネルがつなぎ
輝く上海

How convenient the rail transit is
Bridges and tunnels connect both sides of the Pu River
Dazzling all over the Shanghai City

轨交网络密
大桥隧道跨浦江
光彩耀申城

缪 屹弘
Miao Yihong
age 9
China（中国／上海）

Beautiful lights and colors of the city
Among the skyscrapers
I hide myself in slum

光りかがやく大都会
超高層ビルに囲まれて
わたしはスラム街に隠れる

งามแสงสีเมืองกรุง
ตึกใหญ่โตมองสูงเทียมฟ้า
ฉันซ่อนในสลัม

สุพนิดา เค้าภูเขียว
Supanida Khaophukhiaw
age11
Thailand（タイ）

หัวข้อ : เมือง
งามแสงสีเมืองกรุง
ตึกใหญ่โตมองสูงเทียมฟ้า
ฉันซ่อนใน สลัม

Cathedral belfry
Waiting for Mass to end
A frozen rambler

大聖堂の鐘楼
ミサの終わりを待つ
凍える浮浪者

Katedros varpinė
Laukia mišių pabaigos
Sušalęs valkata

Virgilijus Paužolis
Virgilijus Pauzolis
age12
Lithuania（リトアニア）

In my damp room
With its cracked walls
Lives a picture

湿りを帯びた部屋
ひびの入った壁で
生きる一枚の絵

Nemli odamın
Çatlak duvarlarında
Yaşar bir resim

Topraknur Arslan
age 8
Turkey（トルコ）

外に見える(み)のは
わたしを待(ま)っている街全体(まち ぜん たい)
だから、うふふ

Outside I can see
The whole town waiting for me
So I just smile

Sophie Winter
age11
USA （米国／ダラス）

あかいじてんしゃが
ぼくをのせて
しろいいえのまちへ

My red bike
It takes me to the city
Of white houses

Mi bici roja
Me lleva a la ciudad
De casas blancas

Alejandro Marfil Rodríguez
age 6
Spain （スペイン）

ビルに囲(かこ)まれ
地上(ち じょう)は車(くるま)であふれてる
きれいな空気(くう き)を探(さが)すのは大変(たい へん)

Buildings all around
Too many cars on the ground
Fresh air, hard to find

大廈密滿佈
地面上車水馬龍
難以呼吸到清新空氣

梁 紫彤
Leung Tsz Tung Cathy
age11
China （中国／香港）

This loud town
Even the quiet cat
Watches the cars rush by

■■■■■■■■■■

Isabel Carrick
age14
UK（英国）

このうるさい街(まち)
くつろいでいる猫(ねこ)さえも
通(とお)りすぎる車(くるま)をチラリ

This loud town
Even the quiet cat
watches the cars rush by

店は閉まりかけ
暗い夜道を
僕ひとり

The stores are closing
I walk down the dark street
Alone in the dark night

Les magasins ferment
Je marche dans la rue sombre
Seul dans la nuit noire

Benham Gaspard
age12
France（フランス）

私の街――ジャングル、茂み、森
迷子になった、どこなの、分からない
帰り道が分かるかしら

My city-a jungle, a thicket, a forest
I'm getting lost, losing myself, disappearing
Will I find my way home

Moje miasto-dżungla, gąszcz, las
Gubię się, zatracam, znikam
Czy znajdę drogę do domu

Paulina Ziarek
Pauline Ziarek
age13
Poland（ポーランド）

自転車をこぐ
鳩が
ぼくの肩に

Riding a bike
A pigeon perches
On my shoulder

Andando en bici
Un pichoncito se posa
Sobre mi hombro

Felipe Cuello
age10
Argentina（アルゼンチン）

渋滞中
ビューンと飛んで
無事に家に着けたらなぁ

Waiting in the traffic jam
I want to fly fast
To get home safely

Түгжрэлд түргэн нисмээр
Түвшин амар
Гэртээ харимаар

■■■■■■■■■■

Хулан Жадамба
Khulan Jadamba
age10
Mongolia（モンゴル）

ＪＡＬ財団は、世界三十七の国・地域で十五歳以下の子どもを対象に「世界こどもハイクコンテスト」を開催しています。このコンテストの特長は「五・七・五」の日本語で表現される俳句だけでなく、世界の子どもたちがそれぞれの母語による「三行詩」と自ら描いた絵で、さまざまな情景やそこから得た感動を表現しているところにあります。日本の俳句のように、有季・定型で十七音という形式を厳格に守ることはできませんが、簡潔な言葉に含みを持たせ、読む者の想像をかきたてるという神髄に変わるところはありません。一九九〇年の開始以来、その魅力は国境を越えて着実に浸透し、至近の大会でもガーナとモザンビークが新たに参加するなど、回を追うごとに参加国や地域を増やし、応募していただいた作品数は累計で七十四万点に達しました。

この本は二〇二一年の第十七回大会の応募作品、一万七千六百九十九点の中から優秀作品百六十五点を収録したものです。各地域で入賞した絵とハイクが、世界各国から品川のオフィスに続々と到着し、国際郵便を開封するたびに、さまざまな地域の子どもたちのエネルギーと、教師や保護者の方々の声援が飛び出してくるような感動を覚えます。

自分が詠んだハイクが表彰され、外国語に翻訳され、書籍やWebで広く紹介される体験を経て得られる創作の喜び、自信。世界中の子どもたちが「ハイクコンテスト」という同じステージで、地球が織りなすさまざまな自然現象や人類の営みに目を向け、共通していること・違うことを認識するよい機会となれば、これに勝る喜びはありません。

二〇二二年の今、地理的な国境を巡り紛争が激化し、他者に対する不寛容さにより、多くの命が失われる悲劇を目の当たりにしています。

私どもＪＡＬ財団は、「世界こどもハイクコンテスト」事業を通じて、ささやかであるかもしれませんが、地球規模で未来を拓くことのできる、次世代の「地球人」の育成に貢献したいと願っております。

最後になりますが、新型コロナウイルス感染症でコンテストの運営が難しい中でも、子どもたちの創作活動を精一杯応援し、多くの作品を届けていただいた世界各地の教育者の方々、対面での会議開催が難しい中、選考にあたられた審査員の皆さま、国際俳句交流協会、国際交流基金、日本ユニセフ協会、各国大使館、外務省、在外公館、文化庁、ブロンズ新社、日本航空などの各団体の皆さまに、心より御礼を申し上げます。

公益財団法人 ＪＡＬ財団
常務理事 池田 了一

＊第十八回「世界こどもハイクコンテスト」は、二〇二三年に「家族」をテーマに開催する予定です。世界中の子どもたちからの作品をお待ちしています。詳細は、公益財団法人 ＪＡＬ財団のホームページ（https://www.jal-foundation.or.jp）をご覧ください。

Epilogue

The JAL Foundation holds the World Children's Haiku Contest for children under the age of 15 in 37 countries and regions around the world. The beauty of this contest is not only the haiku written in Japanese consisting of three lines in syllables of five, seven five, but also the three-line poems created by children from all over the world in their native languages and the various scenes and emotions they depict in their drawings. Although it is not possible to adhere strictly to the traditional seasonal, fixed 17-syllable format of Japanese haiku, there is nothing that can change the essence of haiku, which through its brevity, captures the imagination of the reader. Ever since the contest started in 1990, the appeal of haiku has steadily spread beyond national borders, and with Ghana and Mozambique joining in the most recent competition, the number of entries has steadily increased with each passing year, bringing the total number of entries to 740,000.

This book contains 165 of the best entries from the 17,699 entries for the 17th World Children's Haiku Contest held in 2021. Each time I open an international package of prize-winning drawings and haiku in each region that arrive one after another at the Shinagawa office, I am touched by the energy of children from different regions and the support of their teachers and parents.

The joy and confidence that children gain through the experience of creating a haiku, being commended for their work, and having their haiku translated into other languages and widely distributed via books and online; there is no greater joy for the children of the world than being on the same stage of the haiku contest and having an opportunity to see some of the natural phenomena that exist on our planet, learn what everyday life is like in other countries, and recognize the commonalities and differences.

Now, in 2022, we are witnessing the tragedy of many lives being lost due to intolerance shown towards others as conflicts over national borders intensify.

Through the World Children's Haiku Contest, the JAL Foundation, in our own modest way, would like to contribute to the development of the next generation of global citizens who will pioneer the future on a global scale.

In closing, I would like to express my heartfelt gratitude to all educators across the globe who gave their best support to children's creative activities and delivered many works despite the challenges of running the contest during the COVID-19 pandemic, to the judges who made their selection of entries despite the difficulties of holding face-to-face meetings, and to the various organizations that extended their continued support such as the International Haiku Exchange Association, the Japan Foundation, the Japan Committee for UNICEF, embassies of various countries, the Japanese Ministry of Foreign Affairs and diplomatic missions, the Agency for Cultural Affairs, Bronze Publishing Inc., and Japan Airlines.

Ryoichi Ikeda
Managing Director
JAL Foundation

The 18th "World Children's Haiku Contest" will be held in 2023 under the theme of "Family". We look forward to seeing haiku from children all over the world. For more details, please visit the JAL Foundation website. (https://www.jal-foundation.or.jp/)

Netherlands　オランダ
Enzo Winterink　13
Pien Elfrink　66
Jonas Giling　71

Norway/Sweden　ノルウェー／スウェーデン
Mariam Hasan　42

Poland　ポーランド
Antonina Zakaluzna　9
Lena Bernatek　31
Alicia Boczon　35
Pauline Ziarek　78

Portugal　ポルトガル
Rita Pires Ferreira　28
Mariana Filipa Marques Fernandes　30
Leonor Carvalho Henriques　52
Dânia Marques　57
Margarida Isabel Conde Guilherme　58

Romania　ルーマニア
Butnărescu Lasmina　62

Russia　ロシア
Anatoliy Petukhov　20
Mikhail Maskaev　47

Singapore　シンガポール
Ivanka Chantelle Wimalarathne　15
Sim Jia Qi Jesse Christelle　16
Vivienne Crystalynne Elle Lie　23
Leroy Ho Xian Yang　36
Sofya Abdul Aziz　63
Liew Wen Xin　68
Tasha Fu Xuan En　73

Slovenia　スロベニア
Auri Čučnik　7
Neža Sterle　8
Anadin Zahirović　17
Hana Kosmač　27
Tinkara Tušar　52

Spain　スペイン
Triana Fresco Retamosa　10
Carlota Gómez Rebollo　12
Alejandro Gómez Pletea　36
Leonor Jiménez Guzmán　49
Alejandro Marfil Rodríguez　76
Felipe Cuello　78
Saray Pareja Pagán　81,84

Sri Lanka　スリランカ
Thanumi De Silva　23

Taiwan　台湾（台北／高雄）
Wan Wan-Xin　6
Su Yi-Chen　9
Lin Liang-Yu　21
Kuo Han-Tian　24
Guo Cing-Tzu　28
Lee Hsin-Shun　31
Zhang Yu-Han　35
Lin Nina　55
Chen Cecilia　56
Wang Hsin-Che　66
Chuang Jui-Ying　68

Thailand　タイ
Saniya Panakor　3,84
Keamjira Hormruen　12
Warisara Wankra　14
Montree Nanta　64
Supanida Khaophukhiaw　75

Turkey　トルコ
Elif Topac　25
Melis Tapanoglu　43
Adnan Aras Ozyurekoglu　51
Nevra Tekce　54
Defne Tugba Avci　62
Topraknur Arslan　75

UK　英国
Liliana Bonnett　裏表紙 /Back Cover
Samuel Debenham　30

Lydia Scott　54
Amelia Kan　66
Hector Stroud Arzua　70
Isabel Carrick　77

USA　米国（ボストン／シカゴ／ダラス／グアム／ハワイ／サンフランシスコ）
Henry Muranaka　7
Victoria Garcia　9
Corey Bicknell　25
Lino Yamamoto　29
Jessica Vanegas　38
Landen Victoria Y. Devera　38
Joanna Chen　40
Brendan Skehill　44
Isla Lucas　48
Kayla McIntosh　53
Zoey Ng　69
Sophie Winter　76

Vietnam　ベトナム
Nguyen Hoang Quyen　43
Le Phuong Tu　61

ノルウェー大会とスウェーデン大会は共催となりました。
オーストラリア大会とアンゴラ大会は、入選がなかったため作品は掲載されていません。

The Norwegian Contest and The Swedish Contest were co-hosted.
Entries from The Australian Contest and The Angola Contestant are not listed as there were no winning entries.

INDEX

地球歳時記
まちのうた
Impressions of Towns

2023年3月25日　初版第1刷発行

編　者　公益財団法人JAL財団

装　丁　籾山真之(snug.)
編　集　籾山伸子(snug.)
発行者　若月眞知子
発行所　ブロンズ新社
　　　　東京都渋谷区神宮前6-31-15-3B
　　　　03-3498-3272
　　　　https://www.bronze.co.jp/

印　刷　吉原印刷
製　本　難波製本